I0448534

ADA: Know Your Rights

Returning Service Members with Disabilities

Table of Contents

You've been seriously injured while serving on active duty in the U.S. Military -- perhaps you've lost a limb, sustained a traumatic brain injury or spinal cord injury, sustained hearing or vision loss, or are experiencing post traumatic stress disorder (PTSD) -- and now you're back in the States trying to adjust to living with your injury. This publication explains your rights under the Americans with Disabilities Act (ADA) and provides information on where to get assistance.

The ADA is a civil rights law that prohibits discrimination and guarantees that people with disabilities have the same opportunities as everyone else to participate in the mainstream of American life -- to enjoy employment opportunities, to purchase goods and services, and to participate in State and local government programs and services. Modeled after the Civil Rights Act of 1964, which prohibits discrimination on the basis of race, color, religion, sex, or national origin, the ADA is an "equal opportunity" law, not a benefit program entitling you to specific services or financial assistance because of your disability.

The ADA uses different standards than the military and the Department of Veterans Affairs in determining disability status. The ADA covers people with a physical or mental impairment that substantially limits one or more major life activities such as walking, speaking, lifting, hearing, seeing, reading, eating, sleeping, concentrating, or working. Major life activities also include the operation of major bodily functions such as brain, immune system, respiratory, neurological, digestive, and circulatory functions. Businesses and State and local government agencies must take reasonable steps to make it possible for people with disabilities to be their employees or customers.

Obtaining Employment:
What to Expect

The ADA prohibits discrimination against qualified employees or job applicants on the basis of their disability. It covers all employment practices, including the job application process, hiring, advancement, compensation, training, firing, and all other conditions of employment. Under the ADA, employers cannot use eligibility standards or qualifications that unfairly screen out people with disabilities and cannot make speculative assumptions about a person's ability to do a job based on myths, fears, or stereotypes about employees with disabilities (such as unfounded concerns that hiring people with disabilities would mean increased insurance costs or excessive absenteeism).

Additionally, employers must make "reasonable accommodations" for employees with disabilities, which means changing the work environment or job duties to eliminate barriers that keep an individual from being able to perform the essential functions of the job. Employers are not, however, required to make accommodations that would result in an "undue hardship," which means accommodations that would result in significant difficulty or expense. Also, employers are not required to provide accommodations unless an employee requests them. So, if you're a veteran with a hidden disability like PTSD, you can decide whether to reveal the disability and request accommodations. If you don't need accommodations, you don't have to disclose the disability. Employers with fifteen or more employees must comply with these provisions.

Typical examples of reasonable accommodations are:

- Flexible scheduling at a retail store or restaurant, so a sales clerk or cashier with PTSD can attend counseling sessions or an employee with a spinal cord injury who has a lengthy personal care routine in the mornings can start his or her workday later.

- For an employee who has a brain injury, reducing clutter and distractions, providing instructions and information in writing, breaking down complex assignments into small steps, or allowing a job coach on the worksite to help a new employee get settled into the job.

- Specialized equipment for a data-entry operator who has lost an arm, hand, or finger, such as a one-handed keyboard, a large-key keyboard, a touchpad, a trackball, or speech recognition software.

- Making sure materials and equipment are in easy reach for a factory worker who uses a wheelchair.

- Raising an office desk on blocks for a worker who uses a wheelchair, and making sure supplies, materials, and office machines are at a height that is easy to reach and use and are in a location that is not obstructed by partitions, wastebaskets, or other items.

- Allowing more frequent work breaks or providing backup coverage when an employee who has PTSD needs to take a break.

- Providing a stool for a sales clerk who uses crutches so he or she can sit when not serving customers.

- If the employer has an employee parking lot, reserving a parking space close to the entrance for an employee who has difficulty walking because of the loss of a leg, foot, or toe.

- Providing instructions and information in writing for an employee with hearing loss.

- Allowing an employee to bring his or her service animal to work.

- Allowing an employee with tinnitus to play soft background music or sounds to help block out the ringing in his ears.

★ ★ ★

For more information about these provisions or how to file a complaint, see Contact Information on page 22 for the Equal Employment Opportunity Commission. For practical advice on workplace accommodations, see Contact Information for the Job Accommodation Network on page 23.

★ ★ ★

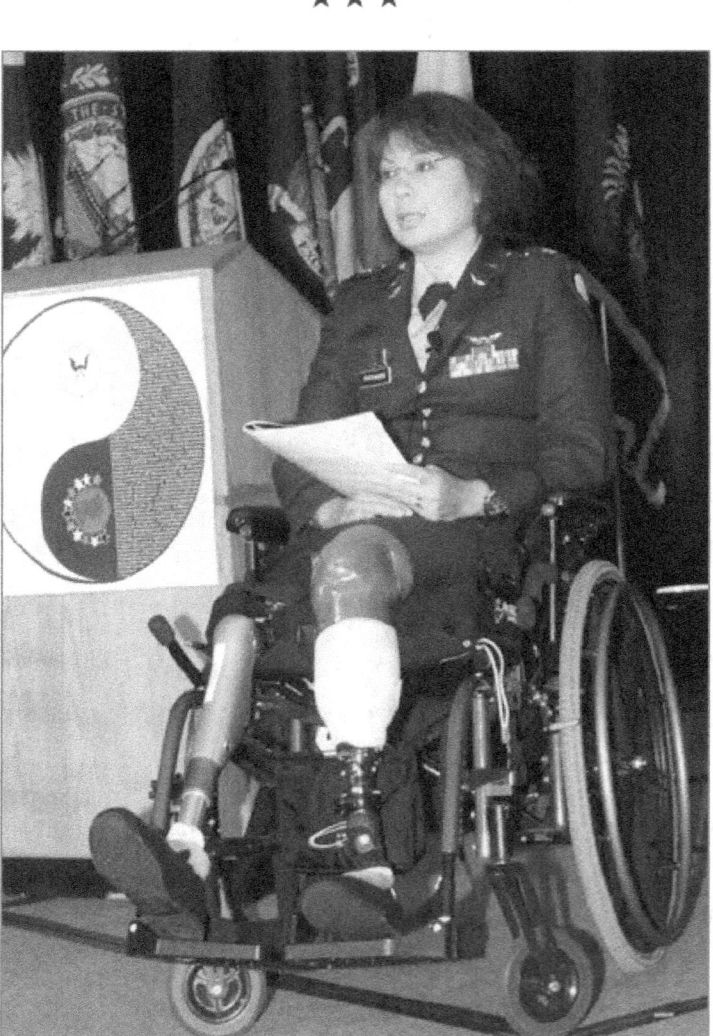

The Hon. L. Tammy Duckworth, Assistant Secretary for Public and Intergovernmental Affairs, Department of Veterans Affairs

Purchasing Goods and Services: What to Expect

There are over seven million businesses in the United States that provide goods or services to the public, including grocery stores, retail stores, restaurants and bars, hotels and motels, gas stations, dry cleaners, laundromats, banks, law offices, medical offices, insurance agencies, movie theaters, art museums, gyms, amusement parks, and other businesses. All businesses that provide goods or services to the public, even small ones with only one or two employees, must comply with the ADA, including the following requirements:

Reasonable Modifications

Businesses must make "reasonable modifications" in their policies, practices, or procedures when necessary so that people with disabilities can be their customers. Businesses are not, however, required to make any changes that would fundamentally alter or change the nature of the business or its services. Additional information about the rules for "reasonable modifications" can be found at www.ada.gov/reachingout/lesson11.htm or by calling the ADA Information Line. See Contact Information on page 23.

Typical examples of reasonable modifications are:

- Modifying a no-pets policy to allow someone with PTSD to bring in a service animal that has been trained to calm the person when he or she has an anxiety attack.

- Modifying a membership policy at a health club to allow a person who uses a wheelchair to bring an aide to provide assistance in getting on and off exercise equipment, in and out of a swimming pool, or to assist with showering and dressing in the locker room, at no additional charge to the club member.

- Instructing staff that if a customer who has lost the use of his or her arms asks them to reach into a shirt or jacket pocket to retrieve the wallet or credit card needed to pay the bill, they should honor the request.

- Modifying procedures at a bank so customers who have difficulty standing for a long time can sit down without losing their place in line.

- Providing refueling assistance at the self-serve price for a customer with a disability who cannot pump his or her own gas.

An example of a fundamental alteration or change is:

- At a gas station with only one employee whose primary job is to protect the cash box or activate the gas pumps remotely, it would be a fundamental change for the employee to leave his or her post unattended in order to pump gas for a customer with a disability.

Effective Communication

Businesses must communicate effectively with customers who have vision, hearing, or speech disabilities. The businesses, not the customers, are responsible for providing the tools or services that are needed for "effective communication." Businesses are not, however, required to provide  any tools or services that would be an "undue burden," which means significant difficulty or expense. The type of tool or service needed depends on the nature of the communication as well as the particular customer's disability. Additional information about the rules for "effective communication" can be found at www.ada.gov/reachingout/lesson21.htm or by calling the ADA Information Line. See Contact Information on page 23.

Examples of effective communication are:

- At a restaurant, the waiter can read the menu to a person with vision loss.

- At a grocery store, a staff person can assist a person with vision loss by locating and retrieving items from the shelves or reading price and content information to him or her.

- At an apartment rental office, the agent can provide a large print copy of a rental contract for a person who has vision loss or an audiotaped or electronic copy for a person who is blind.

- At a retail store, the sales person can write notes to answer simple questions from a customer who is deaf or has hearing loss.

- At a movie theater, staff can provide an assistive listening device for someone who has hearing loss.

- A pizza delivery service must accept calls through the telephone relay service from a customer who uses a TTY because of a speech disability.

New Construction and Alterations

Businesses whose facilities were built or altered since the ADA went into effect must comply with the ADA Standards for Accessible Design so that the facility is accessible to and usable by people who have mobility disabilities as well as people who have sensory disabilities and people who have limited dexterity or grasping ability.

Barrier Removal

In addition, businesses have a continuing obligation to remove architectural barriers when it is "readily achievable" to do so. For example, if inaccessible features in an older facility can be corrected easily and inexpensively, they must be corrected. If there are several inaccessible features and it is not easy and inexpensive to correct them all at once, they should be corrected over time.

When an inaccessible feature cannot be corrected, if there is another easy and inexpensive way to provide service to a customer who cannot access the business, the business must offer that alternative for the customer.

Additional information about the rules for "barrier removal" can be found at www.ada.gov/reachingout/lesson41.htm or by calling the ADA Information Line. See Contact Information on page 23.

Inexpensive steps businesses might take to improve access may include:

- Installing a ramp over a step or two at the main entrance.

- Making a curb cut in the business's side-walk.

- Rearranging tables, chairs, vending machines, display racks, and other furniture to allow for easy passage throughout the business.

- Installing grab bars in a toilet stall.

- Lowering a bathroom's paper towel dispenser.

- Restriping a portion of the parking lot to create accessible parking spaces.

- Installing a paper cup dispenser at an inaccessible water fountain.

Examples of alternative ways to serve a customer when barrier removal is not feasible are:

- At a dry cleaner's, providing curb-side service for a customer dropping off or picking up clothes.

- At a neighborhood restaurant, providing home delivery or carry-out service for a customer who cannot enter the restaurant.

For more information about these provisions or how to file a complaint, see Contact Information on pages 23-24 for the U.S. Department of Justice.

Using State and Local Government Services and Activities: What to Expect

State and local governments offer a wide variety of services and activities that returning service members might need or wish to participate in, and all of these must comply with the ADA. Here are just a few examples of the many types of public services that are covered by the ADA: public trade schools and community colleges, public libraries, public hospitals, public parks and recreational facilities, public transit buses and trains, city and county offices where people go to renew licenses, apply for food stamps, pay their taxes, attend town meetings, serve on boards and commissions, or conduct other government business.

The rules for State and local governments concerning policy modification, effective communication, and facilities built or altered since the ADA went into effect are very similar to the rules for businesses, as described in the previous section of this publication. However, the rules for government facilities that have architectural barriers are different than the rules for businesses. The rules for government facilities are outlined here.

Government offices are not required to make all of their *facilities* accessible, but are required to make all of their *programs* accessible. They can do this by removing barriers at an existing facility, by relocating the program to an accessible facility, or by providing the program in a different manner. Government offices are not, however, required to undertake steps that would result in an "undue burden" or that would fundamentally change the nature of their programs.

Examples of making a program accessible are:

- A community college has two campuses, one is accessible while the other is not. It is not necessary to remove physical barriers at the inaccessible campus, if the two campuses offer the same courses, have the same hours, and serve the same geographic area.

- If the community college offers different courses at its two campuses, offers different programs (for example, day courses at one campus and evening courses at the other), or serves different geographic areas, it must undertake physical improvements at the inaccessible campus or move classes to accessible locations.

- If a person who uses a wheelchair volunteers to serve on a city Parks and Recreation Commission and the Commission's regular meeting place is inaccessible, the Commission must remove barriers at the regular meeting place or relocate its meetings to an accessible location, such as the auditorium of a nearby high school.

An example of providing a program in a different manner is:

- A public library that cannot be made accessible can drop books in the mail and allow them to be returned by mail to accommodate an individual who uses a wheelchair.

An example of an "undue burden" and how it might be solved is:

- In a small municipality, the town council holds its public meetings in an auditorium on the second floor of an historic town building. There is no space on the accessible first floor large enough to hold the meetings, there is no other building where the meetings could be held, and the cost of installing an elevator is beyond the town's financial ability and would destroy the historic features of the town hall. The town's solution may be to install a video conference system in a room on the first floor so people with mobility disabilities can participate in the meetings.

★ ★ ★

If a city or county employs 50 or more people, it is required to have an ADA coordinator. If you encounter problems when trying to use or participate in local government services and activities, you should ask your city or county if it has an ADA coordinator and see if the coordinator can resolve the problem. All State agencies should have an ADA coordinator to resolve problems in accessing State government services and activities.

Contact the U.S. Department of Justice for more information about the ADA or how to file a complaint. For information about the ADA's public transit provisions or how to file a transit-related complaint, contact the U.S. Department of Transportation. For information about the ADA's public education provisions or how to file an education-related complaint, contact the U.S. Department of Education. See Contact Information on pages 23-25.

Other Federal Disability Rights Laws

As noted earlier, the ADA covers employment, access to goods and services, and State and local government programs, activities, and services. There are other Federal disability rights laws that cover housing, air travel, telecommunications, Federal programs and services, and other topics. For more information, see the Department of Justice publication called "A Guide to Disability Rights Laws." You can read or download a copy at www.ada.gov/cguide.pdf or order a copy from the ADA Information Line. See Contact Information on page 23.

Uniformed Services Employment and Reemployment Rights Act

The Uniformed Services Employment and Reemployment Rights Act (USERRA) prohibits discrimination against employees or job applicants on the basis of their military status or military obligations. It also protects the reemployment rights of people who leave civilian jobs to serve in the uniformed services. It applies to all veterans, not just those with service-connected disabilities. Under USERRA, employers must make "reasonable efforts" to help returning employees become qualified for reemployment in the positions they would have attained if they had not left for military duty, or comparable positions. This includes providing training or retraining, at no cost to the veteran. For more information about this law or to file a complaint, see Contact Information on page 25 for the U. S. Department of Labor.

Gen. Hal Hornburg, USAF (Ret), with two service members

A Word about Benefit Programs

You have probably already received information from your service branch or the Department of Veterans Affairs about programs designed to assist returning service members. But you may not know that there are many other benefit programs for people with disabilities, whether you've served in the military or not.

All over the United States there are organizations called Independent Living Centers that provide information about benefit programs and other services for people with disabilities. You can find out how to contact the center nearest you by calling the ADA Information Line or by calling your regional DBTAC - ADA Center. See Contact Information on pages 23 and 25.

State Vocational Rehabilitation agencies also offer services to help people with disabilities enter or return to employment. Your State's contact information is available at www.rehabnetwork. org/directors_contact.htm or from the ADA Information Line.

Publications

The following publications can be ordered by telephone or viewed online.

A Guide to Disability Rights Laws
www.ada.gov/publicat.htm#Anchor-14210
800-514-0301 (voice)
800-514-0383 (TTY)

Americans with Disabilities Act: Questions and Answers
www.ada.gov/q%26aeng02.htm
800-514-0301 (voice)
800-514-0383 (TTY)

The ADA: Your Employment Rights as an Individual With a Disability
www.eeoc.gov/facts/ada18.html
800-669-3362 (voice)
800-800-3302 (TTY)

Veterans with Service-connected Disabilities in the Workplace and the Americans with Disabilities Act (ADA)
www.eeoc.gov/facts/veterans-disabilities.html

Accommodating Service Members and Veterans with PTSD
www.jan.wvu.edu/corner/vol03iss02.htm
800-526-7234 (voice)
877-781-9403 (TTY)

Accommodating Employees with Traumatic Brain Injury
www.americasheroesatwork.gov/accommodatingTBI.html

Accommodating Employees with Post-Traumatic Stress Disorder
www.americasheroesatwork.gov/accommodatingPTSD.html

So You Want to Go Back to School
www.ed.gov/about/offices/list/ocr/letters/back-to-school-2008.html

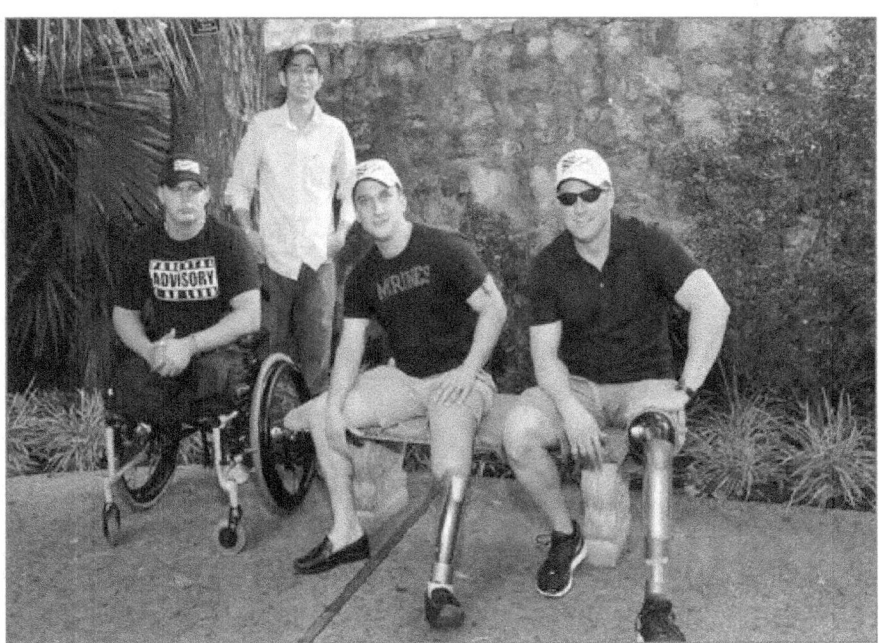

Contact Information

All the agencies listed below provide technical assistance to help businesses, State and local governments, and individuals with disabilities understand the ADA. Each agency specializes in different ADA topics.

The **Equal Employment Opportunity Commission** provides information about the employment provisions of the ADA.

For questions
1-800-669-4000 (voice)
1-800-669-6820 (TTY)

For ordering publications by mail
1-800-669-3362 (voice)
1-800-800-3302 (TTY)

For ordering publications online
www.eeoc.gov/eeoc/publications/index.cfm

Website
www.eeoc.gov/laws/types/disability.cfm

Email address -- info@eeoc.gov
Please include your zipcode and/or city and state so your email will be sent to the appropriate office.

Mail
Please call, or click on the website's link "Contact Us," to get the address for the office that serves your area.

The **Job Accommodation Network** provides information about accommodating employees with disabilities.

800-526-7234 (voice)
800-232-9675 (voice)
304-293-7186 (voice)
877-781-9403 (TTY)
304-293-5407 (fax)

Website
www.jan.wvu.edu

Job Accommodation Network
PO Box 6080
Morgantown, WV 26506-6080

The **U.S. Department of Justice** provides information about the provisions applying to businesses and State and local government agencies, including the ADA Standards for Accessible Design. Contact the ADA Information Line to speak to an ADA Specialist who can answer questions and help you understand the ADA's requirements. All calls are confidential.

ADA Information Line
1-800-514-0301 (voice)
1-800-514-0383 (TTY)
24 hours a day to order publications by mail
M-W, F 9:30 a.m. - 5:30 p.m., Th 12:30 p.m. - 5:30 p.m. (eastern time) to speak with an ADA Specialist.

Website
www.ada.gov

U.S. Department of Justice
Civil Rights Division
950 Pennsylvania Avenue, NW
DRS-NYA
Washington, DC 20530

The **U.S. Department of Transportation** provides
information about the public transit provisions of
the ADA.

ADA Assistance Line
888-446-4511 (voice)
TTY: use relay service

Website
www.fta.dot.gov/ada

E-mail address
FTA.ADAassistance@dot.gov

Federal Transit Administration
East Building
1200 New Jersey Ave, SE
Washington, DC 20590

The **U.S. Department of Education** provides information about the public education provisions of the ADA.

800-421-3481 (voice)
877-521-2172 (TTY)

Website
www.ed.gov/about/offices/list/ocr/index.html

E-mail address -- ocr@ed.gov

Mail
Please call, or click on the website's link "Office Contacts," to get the address for the office that serves your area.

The ten regional **DBTAC - ADA Centers** provide information about the ADA.

800-949-4232 (voice and TTY)

Website
www.adata.org

The **U.S. Department of Labor** provides information about the provisions of USERRA.

202-693-4731 (voice)
TTY: use relay service

Website
www.dol.gov/vets/programs/userra/main.htm

Notes